D0679565

LOVE POEMS
(for the Office)

ALSO BY JOHN KENNEY

Truth in Advertising
Talk to Me
Love Poems for Married People (poetry)
Love Poems for People with Children (poetry)
Love Poems for Anxious People (poetry)

LOVE POEMS

(for the Office)

JOHN KENNEY

G. P. Putnam's Sons / New York

PUTNAM
— EST. 1838 —

G. P. PUTNAM'S SONS
Publishers Since 1838
An imprint of Penguin Random House LLC
penguinrandomhouse.com

Library of Congress Cataloging-in-Publication Data

Names: Kenney, John, author.
Title: Love poems : (for the office) / John Kenney.
Description: New York : G. P. Putnam's Sons, [2020]
Identifiers: LCCN 2020035034 (print) | LCCN 2020035035 (ebook) |
ISBN 9780593190708 (board) | ISBN 9780593190715 (ebook)
Subjects: LCSH: Offices—Poetry. | LCGFT: Poetry.
Classification: LCC PS3611.E6665 L69 2020 (print) |
LCC PS3611.E6665 (ebook) | DDC 811/.6—dc23
LC record available at https://lccn.loc.gov/2020035034
LC ebook record available at https://lccn.loc.gov/2020035035

Printed in the United States of America
1   3   5   7   9   10   8   6   4   2

Book design by Joy O'Meara

For my boss.

Also, I quit.

One of the symptoms of an approaching nervous breakdown is the belief that one's work is terribly important.

BERTRAND RUSSELL

LOVE POEMS

(for the Office)

A Q&A with the author

Q: Your last collection, *Love Poems for Anxious People*, came out at almost the exact same time the coronavirus hit the United States. Now you have *Love Poems for the Office* and many offices are either closed or at least radically changed. Should you stop writing books?

A: That's a great question, and you are not the first person to suggest that (my publisher, friends, readers, my parents).

Q: What will your next untimely book title be?

A: *Love Poems for the Apocalypse.*

Q: I read your previous collection, *Love Poems for Anxious People*.

A: Thank you.

Q: I'm joking. I didn't.

A: Oh.

Q: Why offices?

A: The idea was my editor's. My initial idea, *Love Poems for Middle-Aged Poets Who Wish They Had Gone into Finance Instead of Poetry Because Now They Have Almost No Money in the Bank and Are Royally Screwed* was rejected by my publisher.

Q: Have you ever worked in an office?

A: No, but I've certainly applied many times. As yet, I've not heard back.

Q: What you've done in this book is take the mundane world of the office and turn that world into mundane poems.

A: I think that's exactly right.

Q: You have been called the greatest poet of your generation. What's that like?

A: I have? I hadn't heard that.

Q: Wait. Sorry. That was Mary Oliver who was called the greatest poet of her generation. No one has called you anything except for some very bad names on Goodreads. Want to hear some of them?

A: I'll pass.

Hold the elevator?

If I am honest
I did see you
holding those two coffees
a file wedged under one arm.
Jill, right?
So let me explain what happened there, Jill.
I was kind of in a rush
to get back to my desk, I mean.
Not to a meeting or anything.
Just to eat my lunch
and simply space out
and watch YouTube.
So I had been standing
in that elevator
a good seven seconds
which can feel like a long time in an elevator.
And I'd pressed the close door button
a few times
(maybe ten?)

when I saw you shuffling toward the elevator
smiling
eyes wide
as if to say
Hold the door?
Please don't take this
as a criticism
but you are a slow walker, Jill.
Also the doors had started to close
in large part because I
was pressing the close door button
but making it look like I
was pressing the open door button
while making a face like
How do these crazy buttons work?!!
This is so complicated!
Get the next elevator, Jill.

Zoom calls in the time of coronavirus (part 1)

Mary is sitting on her Peloton
pedaling and talking.
Ben is in his car
waiting to go into a car wash.
Terry is in his daughter's room
surrounded by pink stuffed animals.
Greg is taking a shower
which makes it hard to hear him.
No one cares.
It's Zoom.
Zoom is from the Greek word for
no one gives a fuck anymore.

Shakespeare never used the word "ping" and neither should you

When you say
ping me
I want to punch you.
It's true.
Bio break, too.
It makes me cringe.
And if I am being honest
I don't care about your ducks or the row they're in.
I don't know what net-net means
unless it's being said by an excited tennis announcer.
Come to think of it
let's *not* circle back
or drill down
or take a deep dive
or take it offline
or level the playing field
or create action items
and honestly I don't care

if this won't scale
and may I add that
going forward
I would like to park this project.
And this job.
I quit.
Now.
Sorry.
I have a hard stop.

A review of the office holiday party (from the police report)

The food ran out.
That was the problem.
The booze didn't, though.
That was also part of the problem.
Kissing people was another part of the problem.
In all there were a lot of parts to the overall problem.
Another significant problem was that
I was dancing
alone
(according to eyewitnesses)
and spinning
and singing a song I had made up
Take your pants off!
C'mon, everybody, take your pants off!
And then, according to depositions
I performed a spinning move of such force
that I somehow flung myself
off the dance floor

and into a table
of several women from accounting
who were chatting with the CFO
breaking the table
and then throwing up on myself
and the CFO.
I think that was the main problem.
Still.
Prior to that it was one of the better holiday parties.

Whose meeting is this?

After we had all filed in
found a seat
made some small talk
someone said
I'm sorry but whose meeting is this?

Someone asked if it was Cindy's meeting.
But Cindy said she thought it was Jagdish's meeting.
Jagdish seemed confused and said it was Alan's.
Alan wasn't there so it probably wasn't his meeting.
Gary asked if it could have been a mistake
and then laughed too loud
and got embarrassed and thought about crying but
    didn't.
Jagdish said it couldn't be a mistake, that it was on his
    calendar.
Cindy seemed super annoyed and said
if it was on your calendar to jump off the building would
    you do it, Jagdish?

It got quiet after that
during which everyone wondered
what the point of this meeting was
what the point of any meeting was for that matter
wondered where time went
and why they hadn't done more with their lives.

And as they filed silently out of the room
to allow another meeting in
no one had any idea
how they would account for this
on their time sheet.

Why are you tanned?

At the morning staff meeting someone asked me how I
    was feeling.

I said great.

So you're better, they asked.

Which is when I remembered that I had called in sick
    the day before.

Definitely better, I said. Probably a twenty-four-hour bug.

Was it a tanning bug? someone else asked. Because you
    look tan.

Oh . . . this, I said. Yeah. I had a fever. So it could be that.

Fevers make you tanned?

I said they could, in rare instances.

But someone Googled that quickly and said that wasn't a
    thing.

You know what can make you tan is the sun, someone
    suggested.

On a golf course, someone else added.

I agreed that that was possible.

But you were sick, they said.

I was. I was sick. So I wasn't outside and certainly not on a golf course.

Were you outside on a golf course? they asked.

You can be sick in so many places, I said, though I wasn't sure what I meant.

So I added, You know how you can work from home? Well I have heard that you can be sick on a golf course.

Were you sick on the golf course? they asked.

I was nauseated on the front side, yes. Mostly because of my putting.

I felt much better on the back nine.

Here comes Milo

I quickly pick up the phone
even though it hasn't rung
because Milo is coming.
Uh-huh . . . okay . . . I understand
I say to no one.
Most people would wave
leave
understand.
Not Milo.
Milo leans against the high riser
of my cubicle
biting a nail
smelling it
a man with time on his hands.
He is at work after all.
I point to the phone
hand over the mouthpiece.
What's up, Milo? On a call.
Milo examines all of his fingernails

and I wonder if he has even heard me.
Then he chuckles and says
My weekend was crazy sick.
(It's Wednesday.)
That's great, I say. It's just . . . I have this call.
He moves some files off the chair next to my desk
and then sniffs my half-eaten sandwich.
Who's the call with? Milo asks.
Umm . . . my oncologist, I say.
Cool. I'll wait.

Team building

It had been a long day
of team-building exercises
and I sort of thought
we were on the same page
as to how ridiculous it was.
It turns out we were
not on the same page.
Which may be why
I did not
catch you
during the trust fall.
I thought it would be funny.
And it was.
For me.
Briefly.
I never thought
you would land
so hard.
Or that your head

would make that sound.
Or need two stitches.
Just as I never thought
you would trust me
as I had once trusted you
to give me a raise.
Trust is a funny thing.

Welcome to the group

I am sure
it will be fine
that we are now
working
in the same group
even though
we hooked up
a while back
after an office party
and then went out
a couple of times
but ended badly
and then
hooked up again
when you said
you were leaving
the company
but ended up staying
and we ended badly
again.

Not to mention
I have heard
you are dating someone
from finance now.
How nice.
Also.
That idea
you presented today?
I hated it.

What I would do differently if you weren't my boss

I wouldn't laugh
the next time you tell that joke
about the two nuns
because it's not funny
or even physically possible.
I would just stare at you
as if to say
you're a dickhead.
And then I might say
out loud
You're a dickhead.
And when you came by my cubicle
to ask if I had gotten to that report
even though you could see
that I was eating an egg salad sandwich
only to say
I guess it will have to wait until after your lunch
and make a face
and say how much you hate egg salad

I might say something like
That's funny because I hate your face.
I would say that if you weren't my boss
and I didn't have a mortgage.
And then I might add that your kids are weird-looking.
Because they are.

Who keeps stealing my yogurt?

The first noble truth of Buddhism
is that life is suffering.
And that suffering has a cause.
It's called craving or attachment.
(I should mention here that I am not Buddhist.
I read all that stuff on a Snapple cap once.)
My point is I am suffering
as I was very attached to
my 3 p.m. snack.
You all know this.
And yet even though I have
clearly marked my snacks
(Elaine's snack . . . DO NOT TOUCH!)
you take them.
I think it was you, Greg.
Or possibly Tracy.
I will find out.
That was a Chobani yogurt
you stole
you sons of bitches.

I will go through your trash.
I will find the empty container
which I will then recycle (per company policy).
And then I will exact revenge.
Suffering, indeed.
Coming soon to a cubicle near you.

Open seating

I love the new open seating plan.
I really do.
I love having no idea
where I am going to sit each day.
Or where others are.
The democratic nature of it
that anyone
can sit
anywhere
at any time.
How you can't keep a photo
or a book
or anything for that matter
at your work space
or it is taken away that evening
by the cleaning crew.
The thing is though
I have been sitting
in this seat for, like,

two weeks now.

And I'm not sure why I'm yelling.

But seriously

get the hell out of my seat.

Mythirdemailtotechsupportregardingmyfreaking stickyspacebar

Notsureifyoureceivedmypreviousemails.
Ihaveastickyspacebarandit'smakingmyworkverydifficult.
Isthereanywayyoucouldgetbacktome?
I'matextension6679.
Oremail.
Createaworkorder.
Somesignthatyouareawareoftheproblem.
Becauseitisaproblem.
ClientsarewonderingwhatthehellIam
sayinginmyemails.
Decipheringthemlikeit'ssomekindof
BletchleyParkduringWorldWarIIscenario.
JustanoteontheBletchleyParkthing.
TheyactuallycrackedtheEnigmaCode.
AllI'mlookingforisaloaner!!

Thank you for heating up fish leftovers in the break room microwave again

I am
assuming
it's fish.
Though it certainly
could be
something else.
A dead man's foot
for example
if the smell
is any indication.
Break room's all yours.

You will be missed

This place will not be the same
without you, Wayne.
You're the man.
Do you know that?
I certainly didn't know that.
I just learned that today
from some of the people here
at this very small going-away party
in your office
which I wandered into
after leaving a meeting early
Layoffs are the worst.
I just wanted to say
good luck
finding a new job
especially in this economy.
And also to introduce myself.
And ask if it would be okay
if I took your chair

and that awesome retro joke photo.
Which it turns out
is not a retro joke photo
but your family.
My bad.
Okay to take the chair?

Zoom calls in the time of coronavirus (part 2)

Why yes
that was my five-year-old son
running back and forth
behind me
nude
shouting
Anus! Anus! Anus!
while the dog barked
and my husband yelled
and I leaned away from the computer camera
so no one would hear me shout
*Greg! For Chrissakes, can you get the fucking kids out of
    here?!*
and then smoothly sat back up
only to see the rather stunned faces
of my colleagues
and hear my boss
remind everyone
to mute themselves.

We're in cubicles, Betsy, which means I can hear your phone conversations

You have my sympathy
Betsy
on the strife
in your home life.
But I do not think
that I
or the nine other people
who make up digital marketing
should hear you say
I'm sick of you getting drunk
and peeing in the bed, Alan.
And Alan's response
which you repeated aloud
Oh I'm the one who drives you to drink
was neither kind nor fair.
Though I cannot speak to your
homelife and your ability
to make someone want to drink heavily.
Though I do think Alan may have a point.

. . .

I am sorry
you are not feeling well
Bets.
But here's a thought.
Maybe make that call from home
or the bathroom
or another country.
Because everyone can hear
you tell your (hopefully?) doctor
that you have a burning sensation
when you urinate
which I will grant you
is no fun.

. . .

Sorry
what exactly do you mean
when you say
you've found a good spot
in the woods
to bury the body?
Cat.

Okay then.
Sorry for listening in.
Wait.
Your cat's not dead.

A word of advice to the interns

Please take this in the spirit
with which it is given but
I got sooo hammered last night
might not be something
you want to share
in the elevator.

It may surprise you to learn
that many of us could already sense that
from both your pallor
and the stale smell of
off-gassing booze emanating from your body.

Also, congratulations on
hooking up last night with
a totally hot guy.
All of us hope you're both
very happy in the years to come
should you ever see him again

although that seems unlikely as you
had no idea what his name was.

And thank you for not *puking*
in the elevator
even though *that gross perfume* was killing you.
The (gross) perfume was Susan's
the woman behind you
head of HR.
You'll meet her later today.

Harmless office crush

It's harmless.
And no one knows.
Though I have heard people
might know
by the expression on my face
when you walk into a meeting room
and my voice changes
and I turn red
and blurt out things like
Oh hey, Lynnette,
don't you look impossibly beautiful today.
Which I had not meant to say out loud
nor the follow-up line
Dear God the man who gets to lie next to her at night.
I would like to apologize for that
as company policy prevents me
from commenting on your looks
your gender (should you chose to identify a gender)
or the way the afternoon light hits your hair.

We are simply colleagues.
I get that.
And you are engaged.
But if you have second thoughts
or better yet he happens to die soon
I hope you know that I am here most nights until 7.

No one was paying attention to your presentation

Oh sure
Jen will say
You crushed it, Betty!
But you lost her after slide four
of seventy-three.
What Jen actually did was
pretend to take notes on her phone
and instead buy four pairs of shoes
and a dehumidifier.
Sanjay looked like he was paying attention
but he was scheduling a job interview.
And Ashley
who was wide-eyed and smiling
was replaying last night's episode of
The Great British Bake Off
and briefly sexting with her boyfriend
which was weird to do
during the monthly sales meeting.
Maybe next time crush it in half the number of slides?

Autocorrect

In regard to my recent chain of texts to you.
In no way did I mean
that the cost of the
new shipment would be
penises.
I of course meant peanuts.
I was typing quickly while walking.
Nor did I mean the follow-up text
I've been paying in penises my whole life!
I have no idea what I meant by that.
I was simply trying to make light
of the horror of sending the word "penises"
to you, our senior client.
I thought you might find that funny.
I was wrong.
Penises have no place in marketing.
And may I just say again
that I absolutely do not hope for your
quick death.

I of course meant quick deal.
I do not want your quick death.
Until the time comes for you to die.
I'll stop here.

My boss's six-year-old is at the office for the day

It was cute at first
when he popped his little head in
to say things like
It would be useless if you were a baby and you were in
*   prison*
because you could just crawl through the bars
before running back down to his mother's corner office.
I smiled
and went back to writing a brief
that was proving difficult.
I was finally typing when he burst in to shout
Hey ho my name is Joe my butt is bigger than Mexico
before running off.
He surprised me there
and I spilled coffee on my pants
but I smiled
as the little bastard left.
I waited
staring at the door

for what seemed like minutes.
No return visit.
So I typed.
Until he burst in so fast
that I wet myself a little
as he said
My mom is the boss of you.
He cackled and left.
Children can cackle.
I don't know why I thought
it would be a good idea to
wait by the door
crouched down
and whisper
Your mother is a talentless, narcissistic clown!
But I did.
He was with his mother this time.

Conference call

Sometimes
I think better
when I pace
around my small home office.
So that's what I was doing
when talking through
the Q4 numbers.
I also tend to think better
when I am not wearing pants.
So that's also what I was doing
because I thought
it was a conference call
not a video conference call.
Also dancing.
Because sometimes I think better
when I do a little dance.
And rub my butt
as if I am, say, KC
of KC and the Sunshine Band.

Which is strange for a forty-eight-year-old tax attorney.
My apologies
to the entire team
in all twelve countries.
I hope human resources
and the internal review board
will accept my regrets.

Did you just flush a toilet?

I think it was Jan who asked first
though others on the call
said they were thinking the same thing.
It's just that I had meant to go
before the call
and then the call went
so long.
I thought I had hit mute
but apparently I didn't
and the sound really does carry
in the office bathroom.
And I shouldn't have lied
when Jan asked if I just flushed a toilet.
Wasn't me. Who would do that?
I shouldn't have lied.
I don't normally lie.
That's a lie.
Also.
I didn't realize the rest of you were all

in the same room
around the same table.
Still, super-productive call
everyone agreed
before the peeing thing came up.
Action items to come.

Zoom calls in the time of coronavirus (part 3)

Each of us talked about the past few months.
About what we'd accomplished
With all this time at home.
I can speak French now, I said
And I learned the names
of all eighty-eight constellations
in the night sky.
Also karate. I took up karate. Online class.
The unicycle is fun
if you know how
and I do now.
This is what I have done
with my time
over the past two months
I said.
Wish.
I meant *wish* I had done
with my time
over the past two months

instead of what I did do
which was almost nothing
except wear the same clothes
day after day
eating mocha chip ice cream
for breakfast
and saying things on Zoom calls like
Oh for Chrissakes what's the point?

Office, August, freezing

The thing is
I am wearing a sundress
but also a sweater
a fleece
and a ski hat.
And my fingertips are white
while outside my window
it is 93 degrees and humid.
My understanding is that
we are an insurance company
not a large-scale meat storage facility.
And yet here you come
Gary
plodding down the hall
toward the thermostat
for the third time today.
I see you, Gary.
And I see that you now see me
shivering, staring, glaring.

Turn around, old chum.
Take your high-waisted pants
And mustard-stained golf shirt elsewhere.
And maybe tomorrow
just for fun
you wear a dress.

Passive-aggressive emails (part 1)

Hey, Angela.
Hope this finds you well.
And happy belated birthday.
I saw your party on Instagram.
Looked amazing.
(Thanks for the invite.)
I'm joking, of course.
Anyway.
Just making sure you got my last few emails?
I'm sure you're busy
(birthday plans and all)
but I need you
to review the time sheets
and approve them.
Hate to keep bothering you
but you're holding up payroll.
(Not that any of us need the money.)
Thanks!

Gwen

Passive-aggressive emails (part 2)

Gwen.

I am so sorry.

I'm just seeing this email now.

Turns out it somehow went to my junk mail
(how appropriate . . . kidding!).

You are the *best* to remember my birthday.

The party was probably the single best event I've ever
    been to.

Wish you could have been there.

The time sheets.

I have them here on my desk.

But they're just out of reach (joking again . . . still
    hungover).

Can I get back to you tomorrow?

Or in a few weeks?

Thx!

Angela

Passive-aggressive emails (part 3)

Hey, Angela.
Take your time.
I'll just send out an agency-wide email
and let everyone know that they'll get their
paychecks late.
I'm sure they won't mind.
Try Gatorade for the hangover.
Or AA.

Gwen

Passive-aggressive emails (part 4)

Gwen.

I appreciate you staying on top of me like this.

Your ever-present nagging honestly

keeps me in line.

Don't know where I'd be without it.

Except I'd probably have more time to get back to work

without having to answer all of these (junk) emails!

The time sheets are on your desk.

My assistant returned them two days ago.

You must have overlooked them.

It can happen!

Hope you didn't send out that email yet.

That would look really bad for you.

And I would never want that for you.

Hope it's okay that I've cc'd the agency here.

All the best,

Angela

Consider the tuna sandwich

Standing in line at Pret
yet again
a cold tuna sandwich in one hand
a bag of chips in the other
I got to thinking.
Should I also get a Brownie Bite?
Yes I should.
I also got to thinking about lunch.
About what I have spent.
About the 261 working days in a year.
At about $20 per day.
That's roughly $5,220 a year
Accounting for price inflation.
Now multiply that by the 30 years I've been working.
Roughly $156,000.
If I had invested in the S&P 500
that's upwards of $512,833.
Apparently the line had moved by then
and it had been my turn for a while.

Sir?

The nice young man behind the counter looked worried.

Don't cry.

I said, *Do you know that this tuna sandwich cost me
    $512,000?*

He didn't say anything for a time.

But then he said

Well, like, you're also getting the Brownie Bite.

Reply

What goes through Ted's mind
I wrote to Jerry after the meeting
besides bird shit?
I added an emoji of a bird.
But then felt stupid
so I also added
Like the idea of shortening the shipping time
by warehousing it was such a genius idea.
(Although it was pretty good.)
Then I added an emoji of a baby
because Ted is short.
(Well, we're the same height.)
Then I wrote
You know what they say about managers
who suggest shortening the shipping time . . .
they probably have a tiny penis.
And added another emoji
of a crazy face with eyes crossed,
which I know Jerry loves.

I didn't hear back from Jerry.
I did hear from several other members of the team
including Ted
as I had hit reply all by mistake.
It was probably time
to look for a new job anyway.

Error message

Was it you, Ken,
who left the paper tray empty?
I saw you skulk away
as if you hadn't seen the
F-7 error message
Load paper tray 1.
Prick.
I'd rather give myself a tetanus shot
than load the paper tray
because it always feeds wrong.
So I get an F-9 error message.
Pull the top open, take the sheet out
realign the paper in the tray
hit print.
Get a G-4 error message.
You know what a G-4 is, Ken
you bastard?
Goddamned toner.
You're *such* a dick.

So I find a toner cartridge
remove the old one
get ink on my hands and my crotch
as apparently I leaned against the cartridge by mistake.
I'm ten minutes in now, Ken
you sadistic shithead of a sales rep.
And it doesn't even print.
What does print
is a cover letter and resume.
Yours, Ken.

Note in the kitchen next to the trays of sandwiches and cookies

To my colleagues
who last week
yet again
ignored my note
to not touch the catered lunch
meant for the client meeting
leaving the remains of a frenzied feeding
and the always untouched macaroni salad.
These pristine platters are for
today's new business pitch.
So these sandwiches matter.
Which means I have to trust you.
I'm not saying I've laced one of the sandwiches
and three brownies
with a diarrhea-inducing medicine.
That would be madness.
The kind of thing someone driven to the edge

by colleagues who taunt his platters would do.
Take a sandwich.
I dare you.
You have messed with the wrong Admin.

Annual job review, via Zoom

It was not my understanding
that your mother-in-law
would be on our Zoom call
as I hadn't realized
you were staying with her.
I had hoped
we might have a one-on-one
as I have some very real concerns
about your recent underwhelming performance.
And while I agree with your
mother-in-law that you are
a good boy
I do worry about your lack of output.
As you know, we are instituting
a 20 percent salary cut across the board . . .
I see that your father-in-law is also joining.
I did not know he was in a wheelchair
recovering from hip surgery.
And yes

we all had a good laugh
when he insisted that
the kid deserves a raise.
It's just that
it's making this difficult
with your extended family staring at me.
Would a 10 percent increase be acceptable?
And I see Nana has joined
and suggested 20 percent.

What we're thinking at the IT desk

We are here to help.
Because technology can be complicated.
There are no "dumb" questions.
It's not your job.
It's ours.
What do we know about marketing and finance?
When you walk away with a problem solved
we're happy.
And that's why we're smiling.
And laughing.
When you're out of earshot.
Because we can't believe how dumb
your questions are.
Or that you can't find your IP address.
Or the on button.
Seriously.
Have you ever used a computer before?

Do we really need those magnetic security turnstiles in the lobby?

If I swipe my ID
one more time
and do it wrong
so that the machine
makes that annoying sound
and I smash my thigh
into the metal bars
while I'm carrying
a hot coffee
a buttered roll
and an umbrella
spilling the hot coffee
on my pants
and saying the words
Sonuvabitch!
way too loud
and then add
against my will . . .

Seriously!
We are a dinky little ad agency
not the NSA
as others stare at me thinking
That dude's got issues.
Well . . .
I'm just wondering if the agency
offers a paid sabbatical
and what the co-pay on therapy visits is.

I raise you

My hope is that we
are on the same page
as to my value here
and that you can see
how after five years
a 15 percent raise
is not a lot to ask.
As well as a spot bonus.
I sense we are on different pages,
however, when you say 2 percent.
And no bonus.
I counter with 12 percent
and a small bonus.
You say 2 percent
and zero chance of a bonus.
I suggest 4 percent
and a coupon for breakfast at Denny's.
You agree to the Denny's thing
and suggest 1 percent.

I say what happened to 2 percent?
And you say Denny's happened.
I agree to 1 percent.
But you say,
Let's just stick with Denny's.

**HR's guidance to Howard, who has worked here for
forty-one years**

Babe is not a word we use in this office.

And at no time do we ever comment on a colleague's
    body
and certainly don't say things such as
Boy-oh-boy do you fill that dress out or
that's quite a rack.

We greet each other with a smile and a hello
not the phrase *Come here and give us a kiss.*

Because we recognize the essential dignity of all
    employees,
we recognize and honor that Devin from accounting
    identifies as a woman
so please stop saying *What's up with that guy?*

Finally, we know it's your "catchphrase" when you enter
     a room
but please refrain from shouting *Where're my pants?*

We wish you the best in retirement.

Honest time sheet entries

Arriving at 9 and saying I arrived at 8. One hour.

Sitting for a while and going through my bag, organizing and throwing things out. (Oh look, four ChapSticks.) Thirty minutes.

Sighing. Thirty minutes.

Making a list of the things I have to do. One hour.

Looking out the window and wondering about the meaning of life but also what the point of dieting is and why would Colton dump Hannah on *The Bachelorette*. I hate Colton. A while.

Stopping by a friend's desk to not talk about a project and talk instead about her husband, who is a jackass. Thirty minutes.

Lunch. Ninety minutes. Let's call it two hours.

A Google search about a work project which leads to a YouTube video about a kangaroo who can juggle which leads to a video of "Best Denzel Washington movie moments," which leads to calling my mother from an empty conference room and crying for no reason. Two hours.

A purposeful walk around the office, looking like I have to be somewhere, when mostly it's boredom and a way to increase my steps. Ninety minutes.

A conference call where I don't entirely listen but instead listen to a podcast on mindfulness. One hour.

Meeting with the team on action items for the new project, which were remarkably similar to the meeting we had yesterday to discuss the same thing. Eternity. Call it an hour.

Almost 5:30 in that it's about 4:45 and I have a therapy appointment which is not entirely true as it's a yoga class just to unwind from a stressful day.

Are drinks later with friends billable?

You brought your dog to the office

So hey, Klodet
it looks like someone
shit in the main conference room.
And I know for sure it wasn't me
or any of our clients
as that's something I would have noticed.
So I'm guessing it was your dog
who you've brought to the office
again.
The thing is though
we're not a hipster start-up.
We're a law firm
and your dog
Kareem Abdul Ja-Bark
was just humping our client's leg
in the small conference room.
Only problem is
we don't know how to bill for that.

How many hours did you work?

Carl wants to tell me
how many hours he worked
but first he asks me
how many I worked
so I tell him fifty-nine
as I am hoping this will annoy him
which it does
so he says you're pathetic
and that he worked seventy hours last week
and that he has the time sheets to prove it
so I smile and say that two weeks ago
I worked ninety-one hours but Carl
shakes his head and says that two weeks ago
he worked 110 hours
and I say weren't you out
for two days with the flu
and he says I can kiss his ass
as he still managed to work
from the ER
on a saline drip

so I shrug and say that three months ago
I worked 127 hours during which
I conducted two Zoom meetings
in the delivery room during my wife's
fourteen hours of labor (twins)
to which he gives me the finger and says that he worked
171 hours one week in April
during which his father died
and he had to give both the eulogy
and a presentation to a client
(in the same church)
and I say hey numb nuts that isn't technically possible as
    there are only
168 hours in a week
and Carl says why don't you go die
that he would show me both the time sheet
and his father's ashes
so I say sorry about your father
but at least he's dead, I haven't taken a vacation day in
    sixteen years
to which Carl says he would kill to be dead as he hasn't
    taken a vacation day in his entire life including as a
    child
and I say payroll no longer even prints the word
    "vacation" on my time sheets because there's no point
and Carl says that his dreams

are fully-formed work sessions
that payroll says count as billable hours
and that his greatest hope is that he drops dead at his
    desk
writing a monthly status report
and I don't say anything
because I have to give it to him there.

Returning to the office, returning to normal

I waited fourteen minutes
for an empty elevator
pushing the buttons with rubber gloves.
At the ninth floor an older woman
with a cane tried to get on
but I wouldn't let her
which was more for her than me
but also me.
It's so great to be back
I say
through my mask
twenty-one feet from my nearest colleague
when I get to my desk
which has a taped perimeter around it.
What?! she shouts
coming closer.
Stay back you bastard!
I shout

which I hadn't realized
I was going to say
rubbing Purell onto
my hands, arms, and face.

For my mother

I cannot seem to get it right
this small portrait
of my mother.
I've been trying.

I know details of her life.
But I do not know
cannot know
what she felt.

This child of the Great Depression
oldest of five
telephone operator out of high school
mother to six sons.
The resume of a million American women.
She worked.
Here was an economics genius
stretching her husband's firefighter salary
at Filene's Basement and Big Buy

coupons clipped and S&H Green Stamps pasted
shoes shined and clothes mended.
How many dinners made and baths drawn
stories read and diapers changed
cries soothed and skates tied?

Except I can't seem to get it right
sitting here at the dining room table
on a warm spring evening
and again a few mornings later with coffee
and yet again on a cool Sunday evening
thinking on Sunday evenings with her
watching her favorite TV show
The FBI (in color)
gently rubbing salve into her psoriasis-cracked hands
from all the dishes
all that work.

The smell of lilacs coming through the window
brings me back
the sounds from the TV as my children watch *Inside Out*
bring me back
snippets from a movie about the complexity of emotions
bring me back
to her.
But then most days do.

She died suddenly
at fifty.
I was twelve.
It's just that it kind of ruins you.

You go on
grow up
get a job
get a life
act like a normal person.
A whole person.

You can't really explain to anyone
perhaps not even yourself
how it changes you
defines you
leaves you empty of something essential.
What do you do with that?

You name your daughter after her.
You tell your son stories about her.

The time she drove you to the fancy country club
where your older brothers had caddied.
Off you go, she said.
Work.

It was a Friday and you were ten
and you sat on the caddy bench all day
waiting until you were called
to lug the too-big bag nine holes.

The nice man in the strange clothes
signed your caddy card and
you walked to the pro shop
handed it to the man at the little window
and he handed back a five-dollar bill.
What a thing. What a moment.

You took the dime she gave you
and called her for a ride home.
And while you waited
you walked into the pro shop
a place the caddies rarely went
to the small section for *Ladies*
where among the skirts and putters and pink golf shoes
you saw a yellow plastic bag to hold golf tees.
Yes, you thought. Yes.

And in the car on the way home
you showed her the three dollars.
I thought you said five.
And then you handed over this

worthless thing.
This woman who had never played golf
would never play golf.
No one ever flew her anywhere on a business trip
or put her up in a nice hotel
or paid her expenses.

I love it, she said, smiling.
Her gift to me.

I can't seem to get this right.
I want to keep working on it.
I don't want it to end.
Yes, she would say.
Keep working.

ACKNOWLEDGMENTS

Thank you to my good friends at G. P. Putnam's Sons, especially Sally Kim, Ivan Held, Gaby Mongelli, Ashley Hewlett, Alexis Welby, Ashley McClay, Emily Mlynek, and Katie McKee, all of whom are firm believers in purposefully bad poetry.

Huge thanks to Lynnette Blanche and Klodet Torosian, former colleagues, office mates, trusted advisors, therapists, creative directors who kindly lent their time, edits, and ideas. Couldn't have done it without them.

Trusted readers and dear friends Debbie Kasher and Rick Knief.

Thanks to Lulu & Hewitt, eleven and eight, respectively. It would kill you to get office work?

And my wife, Lissa, who likes to remind me how lucky she feels being married to a poet, as opposed to, say, a successful person.

ABOUT THE AUTHOR

John Kenney is the *New York Times* bestselling author of the humorous poetry collections *Love Poems for Married People, Love Poems for People with Children,* and *Love Poems for Anxious People,* and the novels *Talk to Me* and *Truth in Advertising*, which won the Thurber Prize for American Humor. He has worked for many years as a copywriter. He has also been a contributor to *The New Yorker* since 1999. He lives in Brooklyn, New York.